Original title:
Bark and Ballads

Copyright © 2025 Creative Arts Management OÜ
All rights reserved.

Author: Sophia Kingsley
ISBN HARDBACK: 978-1-80567-162-6
ISBN PAPERBACK: 978-1-80567-461-0

Chants Beneath the Canopy

Squirrels chatter, springing high,
While owls watch with a sleepy eye.
The jolly raccoon dances around,
While nature's laughter is the sound.

Frogs croak out a silly tune,
Bouncing frogs beneath the moon.
The trees swish with a giggle or two,
As critters gather for their debut.

Harmonies of the Whispering Leaves

Leaves are whispering secrets sweet,
While ants march in a tiny fleet.
The breeze stirs up a laughter fit,
As every twig begins to spit.

Chirping crickets keep the beat,
While wandering deer tap their feet.
And squirrels giggle, tail held high,
As a buzzard swoops swiftly by.

Melodies of the Forest Floor

Mushrooms dance on a grassy stage,
While hedgehogs puff with pride and rage.
Each pebble skips a jolly tune,
As butterflies float by quite soon.

Toadstools bounce with glee like spring,
While the weary badger starts to sing.
A tap from a rabbit, a jump from a hare,
In merriment found everywhere.

Sonnet of the Sunlit Glade

In sunlight's embrace, laughter swirls,
As otters glide and the water twirls.
Frolicsome pups in chase align,
Tail-wagging fun, all divine.

With sunbeams painting the forest bright,
Every shadow plays with delight.
Joyful echoes from tree to tree,
As nature's chorus sings with glee.

Whispers of the Canopy

In trees so tall, they giggle and sway,
Leaves whisper gossip, in a breezy ballet.
Squirrels wear hats, thinking they're grand,
While wise old owls hold court, quite unplanned.

A raccoon insists that he's got the best loot,
He shows off his treasures, a well-buried boot.
The sun peeks through, with a wink on its face,
As shadows dance lightly, full of mischievous grace.

Echoes of Woodland Tales

A rabbit recites the latest news,
While hedgehogs giggle, they just can't refuse.
A fox in a waistcoat tells tall tales with flair,
Of cunning and charm, and a prize-winning hare.

The bluebirds tweet tunes of joy and delight,
While crickets provide a chorus at night.
Each twig has a story, each leaf has a laugh,
In the woodland's embrace, you'll find your path.

The Symphony of Twisted Roots

Roots twist and turn in a playful embrace,
They tickle the ground in a grand, silly race.
Mushrooms wear glasses, while ants sing along,
Creating a world where the weird feels like song.

A raccoon conductor waves a twig high,
As foxes dance jigs, top hats on, oh my!
Bouncing to rhythms of laughter and cheer,
In this tangled orchestra, there's nothing to fear.

Serenade of the Ancient Grove

In twisted trunks where the silly things play,
The trees nod their heads as if to say,
'Join us for laughter, let's sing a new rhyme,
With saplings and sprites in a jig for all time!'

The wind blows a melody, sweet and absurd,
As creatures convene, it's simply unheard.
With every chuckle, the petals flip-flop,
In this grove of jesters, the fun never stops.

The Lyric of Laughing Streams

In the woods where giggles flow,
Silly critters steal the show.
Frogs in tuxedos, quite absurd,
Dance with joy, flapping their word.

A squirrel juggles acorns bold,
While the trees share tales retold.
Rivers chuckle, splashing wide,
As breezes join the merry ride.

Elysium of the Enchanted Forest

Where trees wear hats, the sun is bright,
And mushrooms giggle, oh, what a sight!
Fairies play hide-and-seek with glee,
Whispering secrets to an old oak tree.

Gnomes in gardens hold a feast,
With pies that boast of a dancing beast.
Laughter rings through leaf and vine,
In this realm where all things entwine.

The Poem of the Untamed Trail

On a path where shadows prance,
A raccoon invites you for a dance.
He twirls around with all his might,
Wearing a mask, he's quite the sight!

Chipmunks play cards, in leafy nooks,
While owls read stories from ancient books.
The trail confesses with every turn,
Laughter's the flame that forever will burn.

Songs of the Moonlit Orchestra

Under moonbeams, critters convene,
Fiddles made of bark, quite the scene!
Crickets chirp a jazzy tune,
While fireflies flash, a glowing boon.

Rabbits play drums on hollow logs,
Joining the symphony with dancing frogs.
Together they sing of joy and mirth,
Creating harmony, wild and spry on earth.

Melodic Murmurs of Mossy Stones

In the glade where stones sit tight,
Mossy whispers bring delight.
Frogs are crooning in the pond,
Singing tales of days so fond.

Chubby squirrels dance a jig,
Chasing critters small and big.
Every rustle, every sound,
Turns the silence upside down.

Stanzas Among the Ferns

Ferns are swaying, dressed in green,
Join the party, what a scene!
Critters giggle, chasing dreams,
In the sunlight, laughter beams.

Ants parade with tiny bands,
Marching off to distant lands.
Gather 'round, let's make a noise,
Nature's chorus, girls and boys!

Chords of the Woodland Echo

Whistles wind amongst tall trees,
Tickling leaves in summer's breeze.
Beetles tap a little tune,
'Neath the watchful, grinning moon.

Fungi strum their caps in glee,
Dancing bugs in harmony.
Every rustling leaf and bough,
Makes a song, oh listen now!

Verses on the Wind

Breezy whispers float on high,
As the wanderers dance and fly.
Dandelions, bold and round,
Spread their laughter on the ground.

A squirrel's tale goes round and round,
As giggles echo, joy unbound.
Nature's humor, wild and free,
Inviting all to join the spree.

Haikus of the Hidden Hearth

In the cozy nook,
A cat steals the warm spot,
While the fire snores soft.

Toast pops with a cheer,
Socks dance in the warm glow,
Nothing but good cheer.

The kettle sings high,
Teaspoons play a small tune,
Whiskers twitch with dreams.

Candles flicker low,
The mouse plans a grand feast,
But cat steals the show.

Legends of the Leafy Labyrinth

In a maze of green,
Squirrels host a loud feast,
Nuts fly through the air.

Rabbits spin and hop,
Chasing shadows of birds,
While owls roll their eyes.

A wise old raccoon,
With tales from the tallest trees,
Cracks jokes no one gets.

Leaves rustle in glee,
As paths twist and bend anew,
Who knew fun could grow?

Fables in the Forest's Embrace

A porcupine sings,
With needles poised as a bow,
His voice sharp but sweet.

Bears groove on two toes,
In the moonlit disco glade,
A furry ballet.

The fox tells a tale,
Of a chicken wearing socks,
In a hat made of cheese.

Crickets chuckle loud,
As fireflies blink in time,
The forest joins in.

Odes to the Oldest Sentinels

The trees stand so proud,
With knots as wise as old age,
Yet they sway and dance.

Their leaves tell a joke,
About acorns lost in time,
Falling with a thud.

Barking at the sky,
The winds gossip and giggle,
Nature's jesters play.

Roots hug the ground tight,
While the branches tickle clouds,
Old men with young hearts.

Legends of the Leafy Lattice

In the woods where whispers play,
Squirrels chatter, putting on a display.
Trees wear hats of green and gold,
Tales of creatures, silly and bold.

The owl winks from a branch so high,
While rabbits hop, oh me, oh my!
With acorns tossed, a clumsy dance,
Who knew that woods could hold such romance?

A raccoon dreams of a grand buffet,
While chipmunks laugh, 'Oh, more delay!'
Ready for feasts of berries and fun,
In this leafy lattice, joy has begun.

So gather around, let's sing a tune,
Under the smile of the silly moon.
With giggles echoing through the trees,
Let's celebrate nature's whims and tease.

Echoes in the Evergreen Embrace

In the pines where shadows sway,
A deer tries ballet, what a display!
Bouncing joyfully on all four hooves,
Nature's laughter, rhythm and grooves.

The porcupines host a prickly night,
While skunks bring jokes that take flight.
With every giggle, the stars shine bright,
In a woodland concert, pure delight.

Frogs leap high with a croak and a cheer,
Hearts feel lighter, smiles appear.
While fireflies dance like glittering stars,
Nature's party has no bizarre.

So swing your partner, give a twirl,
In this embrace, let joy unfurl.
With echoes of laughter in the trees,
Together we find our harmony and ease.

Poems in the Poplar's Shadow

In the poplar's shade, a squirrel dances,
With acorns in tow, he takes his chances.
A jaunty little jig, with nuts in hand,
He laughs at the folks, who just can't understand.

A bird sings a tune, so bright and clear,
While the dog chases shadows that vanish near.
With every misstep, the park's full of cheer,
As laughter erupts, ringing far and near.

A cat on the fence, looking so sly,
Winks at a butterfly drifting by.
With a leap and a pounce, she lands with glee,
Yet misses her mark, and now we all see!

So gather 'round friends, in the poplar's glow,
For antics abound, with more goofy show.
In this comical space, where whimsy takes flight,
We share in the joy, 'til the fall of the night.

Ballads Born in the Breeze

The wind whispers tales, of the silly and spry,
As a kite takes off, soaring high in the sky.
With a twist and a turn, it's caught in a tree,
Leaving the kids giggling, as they climb with glee.

The flowers all sway, to their own little beat,
While frogs in the pond, throw a wild little cheat.
They croak out their songs, but miss the right note,
Funny faces made, as they guzzle their boat.

A rabbit hops boldly, with style and grace,
Until he trips over, his own fuzzy face.
With a thump and a tumble, he shakes off the dirt,
Then jumps up again, with a sprightly flirt.

So sing out the songs, as we roam through the day,
With laughter and smiles, we'll keep sorrow at bay.
In this breezy place, where fun takes the lead,
We'll dance with the wind, and let every heart heed.

Harmonies of Heartfelt Hibernation

In the cozy nook, where the critters all rest,
A bear snores softly, truly far from his quest.
Dreams of honey jars, in the midst of the night,
While the bees buzz around, giving quite a fright.

The hedgehogs, all snuggled, with spines tucked away,
Tell stories of mischief, they did yesterday.
With giggles and chuckles, as the seasons roll,
Their tales may be tiny, but they bless every soul.

A worm in the soil, sings a lullaby tune,
While the owls hoot softly, reflecting the moon.
It's a wild serenade, from the earth to the sky,
Where the rhythm keeps building, and laughter is nigh.

So let's hibernate, with a wink and a grin,
In this harmony sweet, where the fun can begin.
When winter's all done, and we wake from our dreams,
We'll laugh at the tales, over giggly ice creams!

Tales of Timber and Twilight

In the twilight glow, where the trees start to sway,
A raccoon with style, decides it's buffet day.
With a flick of his paw, he steals from the jar,
While the wise old owl says, "You'll never go far."

The sunset paints colors, so bright and so bold,
While the fox tells a story that never gets old.
He chuckles and winks, with a mischievous dart,
As the night wraps around, like a sneaky old tart.

At the riverbank side, frogs think they can dance,
But each little leap, turns into mishap and chance.
With plops and with splashes, their moves go awry,
They land in a puddle, under twilight sky.

So gather, my friends, as the fireflies light,
These tales of the woods, wrapped in laughter's delight.
In the timber we share, where all creatures play,
We'll weave our own stories, in the dusk's gentle sway.

Rhapsody of the Rooted Requiem

In the shade where squirrels dance,
Chasing nuts, they take a chance,
Leaves of laughter, rustling tunes,
Nature's jest beneath the moons.

Rabbits hop with wild delight,
Chasing shadows in soft light,
The old oak chuckles at the scene,
As birds join in, a feathered team.

Worms throw parties underground,
Yet no one knows, they're rarely found,
Roots whisper secrets, deep and low,
While blossoms giggle, putting on a show.

In this grove, let jokes abound,
Where nature's wits are tightly wound,
From laughing leaves to playful breeze,
Life's a jest among the trees.

Narratives from the Nestled Nook

In a corner where shadows lay,
A chipmunk's tale comes out to play,
With acorns stacked like pyramids,
He welcomes pals with silly skids.

A wise old owl yawns, then cracked,
Says, 'What's the fuss? I'll get my snacks!'
While down below, a frog in glee,
Regales tales of jumping spree.

The cuckoo sings a funny tune,
While ants parade beneath the moon,
Each little creature plays a part,
Crafting stories with silly heart.

So gather round, dear critters all,
In this nook, there's room for all,
With laughter ringing, bright and clear,
Nature's humor we endear.

Harmonies of the Hushed Habitat

In the quiet of the glade,
Where mischief hides in every shade,
A skunk sits back, an artist proud,
Creating scents that draw a crowd.

The hedgehog rolls, a prickly ball,
But laughs inside, enjoying all,
With butterflies that tease and flit,
No one can resist their wit.

Among the ferns, a snake will slide,
With jokes that make the crickets hide,
While sunbeams bounce from leaf to leaf,
In this hush, there's boundless grief.

So let us sing, in silly cheer,
Our chorus loud, for all to hear,
In every nook, small wonders sprout,
Humor blooms, there's never doubt.

Fables of the Fragrant Forest

In a forest, lush and bright,
Where pine trees giggle in pure delight,
A raccoon's scheme goes awry,
As he stumbles in a pie, oh my!

The flowers burst in fits of glee,
As bees hum tunes, oh so free,
While mushrooms nod their silly heads,
Creating paths with crazy spreads.

The foxes play hide-and-seek,
With clever puns and little squeaks,
Every rustle, a tale unfolds,
Of merry days and bright, bold goes.

So join the fun, don't miss the call,
In fragrant woods, there's joy for all,
With every twist, a laugh will share,
In nature's fables, love and care.

Melodic Murmurs of Mossy Paths

In the woods where laughter grows,
Singing leaves in breezy shows,
Squirrels dance with nuts in tow,
Nature's jesters steal the show.

Mushrooms wear their polka dots,
Telling tales of silly spots,
While the owl hoots in delight,
As night falls in gentle light.

Anthems of the Autumnal Air

Crisp leaves crunch beneath our feet,
Squirrels throw a nutty beat,
The pumpkin grins, a funny face,
As shadows waltz in playful grace.

Scarecrows sway with charming flair,
Human forms in windswept hair,
Jackets snug, we leap and bound,
As autumn's giggles swirl around.

Whispers of the Water's Edge

Rippling waves in whispers tease,
Frogs croak jokes with utmost ease,
A fish flips up, a splashy pun,
Nature's jest—a splashy run.

Dragonflies in costumes zoom,
Gaudy colors, vibrant bloom,
Turtles laugh in slow parade,
While the reeds sway in charade.

Echoes of the Enchanted Earth

The mountains giggle, peaks so tall,
Echoing in a merry call,
Dancing shadows come alive,
With every step, the spirits thrive.

Rivers chuckle, flowing free,
Tickling rocks in harmony,
Each ripple sings a silly rhyme,
In this realm, we lose all time.

Rhymes in the Radiant Realm

In a land where laughter grows,
The sun tickles all the toes.
Jesters dance with glee and flair,
Squirrels giggle without a care.

Flowers wear hats made of spice,
While rabbits joke about their vice.
The sky twirls in colors bright,
As frogs croon tunes into the night.

Clouds puff up like cotton treats,
While birds perform their silly feats.
Every breeze hums a quirky tune,
Making flowers sway like it's June.

Join in the fun, don't be shy,
Let your spirit bounce and fly.
In this realm where joy's the king,
Every heart is sure to sing.

Ballads of the Bursting Buds

Once upon a time, who knew?
The daisies played peek-a-boo.
Tulips laughed in bright parade,
While violets waltzed in the shade.

A bumblebee was quite the clown,
Buzzing jokes with a silly frown.
He tripped on petals, oh what fun,
While shouting, "Look! I'm number one!"

Every bloom had stories to tell,
Of thunder's laugh and rain's sweet spell.
With giggles spreading through the air,
The garden's joy was everywhere.

So let us strut with leafy shoes,
And pick up all those playful cues.
In this world of burgeoning cheer,
Laughter blossoms all the year.

Chronicles of the Canopy's Call

Underneath the leafy dome,
Squirrels chatter, feeling home.
With acorns flying, nuts abound,
Their antics echo all around.

Parrots squawk in silly tones,
While owls chuckle on their thrones.
The branches sway with stories grand,
As laughter fills this woodland land.

A raccoon, dressed like a star,
Creeps at night, never too far.
He juggles berries with great flair,
And leaves the forest in a scare!

Nature's jesters, bold and free,
Join the dance, come laugh with me!
In the canopy where dreams take flight,
Laughter echoes through the night.

Murmurs from the Mountain's Mist

Amid the peaks where whispers glide,
A llama twirls, a merry ride.
His woolly coat, a fluffy mess,
But dancing is his true success.

The mountain goats swing in a band,
Leaping high, oh so unplanned.
They tumble down, a playful show,
Making friends with rocks below.

Fog rolls in with a giggly sigh,
As chipmunks race and try to fly.
Their tiny voices, sharp and keen,
Turn every stroll into a scene.

So gather round, let voices sing,
In the mountains, joy's the thing.
With every laugh and playful twist,
Adventure waits in morning mist.

Songs of Scarlet Sunsets

In the twilight, shadows prance,
Trees tickle the sky, join the dance.
Squirrels plotting nutty schemes,
Chasing dreams in their wild beams.

Breezes hum a jolly tune,
While crickets croon beneath the moon.
Fireflies blink like tiny stars,
As laughter echoes near and far.

A dog leaps high, with heart so bold,
Chasing tail, or so I'm told.
Puppy paws in playful plight,
Bounding off into the night.

Beneath the glow of sunset's hue,
Life's a jest, it's true, it's true!
With every giggle, joy takes wing,
Tune in to what the critters sing.

Whispered Wishes from the Woodlands

In the glade where tall trees sway,
A fox decides to have his say.
He spins tales, quite the storyteller,
Mice sit round, all held together.

Toadstools listen, growing wide,
While darts fly by, all in good pride.
A dance-off starts, all in good fun,
Hopping high, till the day is done.

Fairies giggle, toss confetti,
Wishing wells are far from petty.
With each splash, a wish takes flight,
Making dreams out of sheer delight.

In this haven, laughter's free,
Nature's gag, it's plain to see.
So if you roam where whispers sing,
You might find joy in everything.

Melodies of the Mellow Meadow

In a field where daisies wink,
Butterflies join the band, I think.
A breeze carries tunes so sweet,
Grasshoppers hop to the happy beat.

Cows in chorus, moo in time,
Bouncing to the joyful rhyme.
A calico cat in fancy dress,
Struts and prances, oh what a mess!

Dandelions puff with glee,
Sending wishes from A to Z.
A rabbit hops with a cheeky grin,
Searching for the best carrot kin.

As the sun dips low to rest,
Nature's symphony is truly best.
So hum along, with hearts full bright,
In the mellow meadow's light.

Odysseys Under the Open Sky

Stars awake with a wink and wink,
As travelers stop, take time to think.
A raccoon leads with a dazzling map,
While owls hoot, cultured chap.

With each step, adventure calls,
Through the forest and over the walls.
A snicker behind each bush and tree,
Mysteries hide, come check and see!

A picnic launched, with pies galore,
Ants march in, they want some more.
A squirrel juggles acorns on cue,
Life's a circus, oh yes it's true!

So let your heart take flight tonight,
Enjoy the journey, what a delight!
With mischief brewing all around,
Wonders await in every sound.

Rhythms of the Rustling Leaves

In the breeze, leaves twist and twirl,
A dance of green, in a joyful whirl.
Squirrels giggle as acorns fall,
Nature's jest, can't help but enthrall.

Breezy whispers tickle my ear,
Tree trunks chuckle, drawing me near.
The sunbeams play on the forest floor,
As laughter rings from every door.

Each rustling leaf has a joke to share,
With each footstep, I'm caught unaware.
The shadows stretch, they're in on the fun,
Turning the day into a playful run.

Oh, laugh with me in this leafy hall,
Where tree spirits whisper and laughter calls.
Nature's comedy, wild and free,
In the rustling leaves, it's a jubilee.

Serenade of the Shaded Glade

Beneath the boughs, a shadowy dance,
A gathering spot for whimsy's chance.
The sun peeks through, a cheeky grin,
While critters conspire to pull me in.

A rabbit hops with a mischievous look,
Almost as if he's read my book.
He winks at the fox, a playful prank,
In this glade, there's mischief to flank.

The brook bubbles over with giggling fish,
Each splash a gleeful, watery wish.
With frogs playing tunes on old lily pads,
Nature's orchestra, none can be mad.

Oh, join the fun in this shady retreat,
Where laughter and joy are light on their feet.
Every tree holds a story to share,
In this glade of shade, laughter fills the air.

Songs of the Perishing Pines

The old pines creak with a jolly tune,
Swaying gently to the light of the moon.
Whispers of humor hide in their scent,
Where pinecones fall like a clumsy lament.

Their needles quiver in a playful breeze,
Tickling branches with giggles and tease.
A squirrel slips on a needle-tipped slide,
Nature's amusement, there's nowhere to hide.

Each branch a stage, so full of surprise,
With antics and flaps, oh how they rise!
The forest erupts with snickers and glee,
As the pines tell tales of their wild spree.

So let's sing along with the pine's hoot,
In the woodland theatre, a gathering to boot.
With every rustle, a laugh we'll find,
In the melodies of trees, joy intertwined.

Lullabies of the Ancient Oaks

Under the oaks, so sturdy and wise,
A gathering spot for the smallest of spies.
The acorns drop with a comical plop,
As woodland critters gather non-stop.

With gnarled branches carrying stories old,
In soft whispers of humor, legends unfold.
The owls hoot in a most charming tune,
Inviting the stars to join their monsoon.

Each knot in the bark holds secrets and more,
While mice dance around on the leafy floor.
The light flickers soft, like a well-told joke,
In the heart of the forest, where laughter awoke.

So come, find solace where laughter's the key,
Under the oaks, where the world's light and free.
Each lullaby sung is a joyful embrace,
In the dappled shade, we all find our place.

Lullabies of the Leafy Ledge

When squirrels sing of acorn dreams,
And sunbeams dance with giggling beams.
The leaves laugh lightly, swaying wide,
As nature's humor can't be denied.

A hedgehog winks, a robin grins,
While butterflies perform their spins.
The breeze plays tricks, a ticklish tease,
As flowers burst with chuckles and squeaks.

The trees tell tales of wobbly feet,
While ants march by with rhythm and beat.
A rabbit hops in silly loops,
While crickets join in raucous groups.

So rest your head on mossy beds,
And dream of laughter, joy that spreads.
In leafy hedges, giggles soar,
As nighttime whispers funny lore.

Echoes from the Enigmatic Evergreen

In a forest where the shadows play,
The Pines tell jokes in their own way.
With pinecone props and leafy hats,
They throw a show while the owl chats.

Squirrels snicker at the jokes so slick,
As branches sway with a playful flick.
The ferns all wiggle, the flowers cheer,
Echoing laughter that you can hear.

The wind brings whispers of goofy tales,
With rustling leaves in friendly gales.
Each tiny twig holds secrets bright,
Of woodland wonders that tickle the night.

So listen close to this merry scene,
Where giggles rip through spaces green.
The evergreens hold a jolly show,
In a landscape where funny vibes flow.

Serenades of the Silvery Stream

The water hums a bubbly tune,
Where frogs embrace a midnight moon.
With dragonfly dancers in a swirl,
The stream sings jokes that twirl and twirl.

Rocky banks, they giggle away,
As fish do flips in a splashy play.
The bubbles giggle, tickled bright,
In this liquid stage of pure delight.

A turtle grins, takes a bow real slow,
As minnows wiggle, stealing the show.
The reeds rock out with rustling cheer,
While frogs croak punchlines in your ear.

So sit by the stream where the laughter flows,
Where every wave a funny story shows.
In nature's choir, let joy cascade,
A serenade where fun is made.

Whispers from the Wandering Wild

Among the bushes where critters dwell,
The wild reveals its comedic spell.
With startled deer and chubby bears,
Nature's quirks are beyond compares.

A raccoon laughs, his mask a guise,
As hedgehogs grin with pricked surprise.
The bunnies hop in syncopated beats,
While the porcupine offers seats.

The owls hoot their nighttime jokes,
As fireflies twinkle, delighting folks.
Each shadow dances in playful jest,
As the forest spins its humorous quest.

So roam the paths, let laughter guide,
In the wandering wild where funny hides.
Embrace the whimsy, let joy collide,
In this lively land where glee resides.

Tales from the Treetop Symphony

The squirrels play drums on the nuts they find,
With acorns flying, they're truly unconfined.
Chirps of the sparrows, a mixed-up tune,
While branches sway softly under the moon.

A raccoon leads the dance with a silly spin,
While frogs in the pond try to join in the din.
Laughter abounds when the owl hoots loud,
As nature's performers entertain the crowd.

A breeze tosses leaves, they shimmy and shake,
While bees buzz around, making quite the quake.
With twirls and leaps, the branches do sway,
As critters put on quite the wild array.

The night rolls on, filled with joyful cheer,
From the top of the trees, we hear the fun near.
In this symphony grand, we all play a part,
With laughter and music that fills every heart.

Rhythms of the Rustling Reeds

The tall reeds whistle a tune in the breeze,
As frogs hop along with the sway of the trees.
Dragonflies dart like they're dancing a jig,
While fish do a flip, making ripples so big.

A catfish croons low, the melody's sweet,
And turtles tap dance with their webbed little feet.
Marshmallows float on the water with grace,
As crickets join in, setting quite the pace.

The reeds rustle softly with secrets they keep,
While snapping turtles giggle and quietly creep.
Each splash a note in this watery show,
As laughter and melodies constantly flow.

The sun's golden rays spill down like a song,
Creating a stage where the critters belong.
Let the rhythms continue, let no one despair,
For in this green haven, there's joy everywhere.

Harmonies from the Hollow Heart

In the hollow of trees, a concert unfolds,
With whispering winds weaving stories quite bold.
The woodpecker drums on the trunk with a beat,
As leaves clap their hands to the woodland's great feat.

A rabbit hops in with a skip and a bounce,
While butterflies twirl in a delicate flounce.
The hedgehog joins in, with a grin oh-so-wide,
While the badger chimes in with a song full of pride.

The echoes resound through the forest of cheer,
As promises linger and laughter draws near.
With each tapping foot and fluttering wing,
The hollow heart's chorus begins to sing.

So gather around, let's embrace the delight,
In this symphony sweet under cool moonlight.
We'll dance with the shadows that flit all about,
As the melodies swell, we'll sing and shout!

Sonnets in the Swaying Shade

In the shade where the branches weave tales of fun,
 Laughter echoes brightly, mixing with the sun.
 A playful breeze tosses leaves through the air,
 While shadows break down into rhythms so rare.

The silly old goat struts with a grin on his face,
 As critters around him pick up the pace.
 A chorus of chirps fills the cool afternoon,
 As nature's own choir sings a whimsical tune.

Under tangled vines, it's a dance quite absurd,
 With moments of laughter, a joy to be heard.
 The twilight descends like a curtain of gold,
 As nighttime begins, more stories unfold.

So let's twirl and laugh from the shade of the trees,
 For life's but a song, with sweet melodies.
 Embrace every moment, let cheer fill each day,
 In this merry realm, come and join in the play!

Reflections of the Rooted Realm

In the grove where shadows play,
Laughter dances in the sway,
A squirrel mocks the passing breeze,
While flowers giggle at the trees.

Underneath the old oak's shade,
Witty whispers softly fade,
A worm tells tales of yesteryears,
While rooting for the buzzing cheers.

Beetles race on leafy lanes,
Chasing tunes of summer rains,
Each trunk holds secrets of delight,
Tickling roots 'neath the soft moonlight.

In this realm of green and glee,
Nature hums her quirky spree,
Each nook and cranny sings a tune,
Of joy beneath the silver moon.

Echoes of the Elders' Wisdom

Grandma tree with bark so wise,
Tells of clouds and sunny skies,
Her branches spread like gossip's arms,
Caressing earth with ancient charms.

A raccoon peers with playful eyes,
Dreams of moonlit pastry pies,
While owls chuckle, deep in thought,
At all the mischief nature's wrought.

Caterpillars roll in mirth,
Spinning dreams of their rebirth,
Profound words 'neath rustling leaves,
Encourage us to dance and weave.

The crickets chirp their nightly calls,
Reflecting wisdom in their brawls,
Nature's jesters, bold and bright,
Spark laughter in the starry night.

Fables from the Flora's Embrace

Petals prance in sunny spots,
Whispers mingle, tie in knots,
A daisy sneezes, pollen flies,
While nearby cacti roll their eyes.

The vines engage in playful fights,
Tug-of-war under twinkling lights,
As mushrooms giggle, round and stout,
Promising fun with every shout.

Bees craft bars of golden honey,
In their hive, it's all quite funny,
With tiny parties, buzzing loud,
Celebrating life, so very proud.

The forest hums a jaunty tune,
Bouncing joyfully to the moon,
Every leaf a laughing sound,
In this embrace, we're all spellbound.

Verse of the Verdant Vault

In the secret of the green,
Mysteries of giggles glean,
Little sprites in mossy shoes,
Paint the wild with playful blues.

The ferns wiggle in delight,
While mushrooms dance in the night,
Frisky foxes under stars,
Swap their stories with the cars.

Bamboo sways with comic grace,
Hosting bamboo yoga space,
As nearby flowers laugh in rows,
Sharing tales of how life flows.

The willow leans with knowing grin,
Laughing at the world's chagrin,
In this vault where laughter's spun,
Nature's comedy has just begun.

Whistles of the Woodland Creatures

A squirrel tried to sing a tune,
But swallowed too much acorn too soon.
The rabbits laughed, they rolled in glee,
While the owl hooted, 'Just let it be!'

The hedgehog danced with twinkling eyes,
Tripping over mushrooms, to everyone's surprise.
The raccoons joined, with a drum made of leaves,
Creating a rhythm no one believes!

A chorus of chirps from crickets nearby,
Echoed in harmony beneath the sky.
The deer pranced around, quite out of time,
Yet everyone giggled, and it all felt sublime.

The forest was filled with nature's cheer,
As every critter showed off their sheer.
With every note, the woods came alive,
In a contagious joy, they all did thrive.

Tales of Twisted Trunks

Once a tree claimed it could wear a hat,
But a twist and a turn made it just look flat.
The birds all chuckled, sitting so proud,
At the tree with gnarled limbs, striking and loud.

A beaver thought he could cut it a crown,
But ended up wearing the branches down.
The fox came by, with a wink and a grin,
'Let's make a party, and invite all our kin!'

So under the branches, they gathered 'round,
With laughter erupting, an outrageous sound.
The tree just sighed, with a creaky old sway,
Guess it's a hat now, hip hip hooray!

Squirrels served nuts in acorn-made bowls,
While shy little mice stole the show with their rolls.
With twisted tales of who wore what right,
The forest became a grand dress-up night!

Whispers of the Whispering Woods

In the woods where secrets swirl and sway,
A tree whispered, 'Do you want to play?'
The breeze chimed in, with a cheeky giggle,
While the frogs croaked back, doing a jiggle.

A shadow approached, it was a clumsy deer,
Tripped on a root, causing quite the cheer.
The trees exchanged glances, a playful debate,
'Does the deer not know it's a dance party fate?'

An owl swooped down, a judge of the fun,
With a feather held high, he declared everyone.
The branches shook laughter, leaves tickled the light,
Who knew the whispering woods were so bright?

So join the tumult where laughter entwines,
With stories of critters and make-shift designs.
Each rustle and murmur, a melody sweet,
In these woods of whispers, there's joy on repeat!

Echoes Beneath the Canopy

Beneath the tall trees, a chatter took flight,
Echoing giggles that danced in delight.
A turtle recited the worst kind of joke,
Until even the stones began to revoke!

A raccoon held court, with loot to display,
Claiming shiny treasures from trash day.
All creatures gathered, their eyes wide and bright,
For a showcase of blunders that felt just right.

The chattering chipmunks composed a tune,
That echoed so loud, it scared off the moon.
With laughter and tunes ringing sweet through the glade,
They found in each echo, the best of parades.

So join in the fun, let your spirits roam free,
In the canopy's shadows, there's mischief for thee.
As echoes bounce back, share stories and cheer,
For beneath all those branches, pure joy draws us near!

Rhythms in the Rushing River

A frog sings loud near the shore,
With a croak that shakes the floor.
The fish swim by with a splashy grin,
While turtles bob, just taking it in.

A squirrel dives for a daring dive,
In water so cold, it makes him jive.
He surfaces quick, now fully awake,
Searching for snacks, for goodness' sake!

The water wheel spins, it clinks and clanks,
As ducks parade in their silly pranks.
With feathers fluffed, they strut and sway,
Making all the fish think it's their play day!

Oh, the laughter rings, as bubbles rise,
While dragonflies dance, oh my, what a surprise!
The river sings tunes of splashes and splats,
In this lively world, with critters and chats.

Lyrics Under the Lilac Sky

A butterfly flutters with flair and style,
On a flower's petal, it takes a while.
With colors bright, it twirls and dips,
Creating art in the air, like fun little flips.

The bees buzz in, with a sticky thread,
Making sure all the petals are fed.
They chat in hums, with gossip to share,
About the flowers, with pollen to spare!

The breeze carries whispers, soft as a song,
While the daisies sway, oh, they can't go wrong!
Each little bloom spreads giggles of cheer,
While nature laughs loudly, for all to hear.

The lilac sky paints a backdrop bright,
As day dreams turn into playful night.
With crickets chirping their nightly calls,
It's a symphony held in charming brawls.

Songs of Sunlight Filtering Through

The sunbeams peek through leafy seams,
Tickling shadows, igniting dreams.
With golden rays, it plays a tune,
While daisies sway in the sun's cocoon.

A chipmunk scuttles, all quick and spry,
Chasing reflections, oh my, oh my!
He stops for a moment, adjusts his hat,
With a cheeky grin, he says, "How about that?"

The leaves rustle softly, a giggly fleet,
As squirrels have meetings to gossip and greet.
"Did you see Benny? He tried to be brave!"
But slipped on a nut, oh the chaos it gave!

Beneath the sun's watch, the laughter rings clear,
In a playground of nature, we hold dear.
With every flicker and gleam that breaks through,
It's a jubilant song that whispers, "Woo-hoo!"

Verses of the Verdant Whisper

In the heart of green, where giggles bloom,
Nature conducts its joyous tune.
With leafy pages that flutter and flow,
Each rustling sound puts on a show.

The rabbits bounce with mischievous glee,
Hopping in time to a rhythm carefree.
They plot and plan, with costumes in tow,
For a wacky parade that steals the show!

A toadstool stage, a crown made of lace,
With lilies playing the trumpet in grace.
An owl brings wisdom, a wonky wink,
As crickets provide the music—don't blink!

The moon peeks down, with a smile so wide,
As the night grows bright with a joyful tide.
All join the fest, in nature's delight,
In verses of green, near the stars' loving light.

Treetop Trills and Thickets

In the treetops, where squirrels dance,
A cat looks up, hoping for a chance.
Branches sway, a dizzying sight,
While birds chirp tunes, oh what a flight!

Leaves giggle in the gentle breeze,
As raccoons plot their cheeky schemes.
Beneath them, frogs croak their loudest jokes,
While rabbits plot to steal some pokes!

A butterfly flits on a whimsy trail,
Dodging a bee who's chasing a pail.
The trees all whisper, a playful crowd,
As laughter swells, echoing loud!

In this thicket, with such delight,
Every critter shines so bright.
They sing and leap, what a merry sight,
In this woodland of sheer delight!

The Ballad of the Wandering Roots

Oh, roots that wander and sway with ease,
Tangled tales dance upon the trees.
They whisper secrets to the soil deep,
While playful shadows tease and leap.

Caterpillars craft their silky dreams,
While ants march busy, or so it seems.
A fox tells tales of skies so blue,
As gnarled branches tickle dew.

Each twist and turn a comical plight,
With laughter echoing into the night.
Their stories weave through leaf and dirt,
A merry band in nature's shirt!

So join the roots, let your spirit frolic,
In a tale of whimsy and pure symbolic.
For every step sings of joy anew,
In this lively dance of cheer for you!

Harmonics of the Twilight Grove

In twilight's glow, the wee ones gather,
As fireflies dance in a joyful lather.
Crickets chirp a comedic tune,
While owls laugh at the brightening moon.

The trees hum softly, their branches sway,
In this merry grove, come what may.
Frogs croak chorus in silly style,
As shadows prance with every smile.

Each note a giggle, each rustle a cheer,
As friends unite, drawing near.
In the twilight, so full of glee,
Nature's orchestra plays wild and free!

So lift your voice, be one with the night,
Find humor in every fleeting sight.
For here in the grove, all troubles cease,
And laughter echoes, bringing peace!

Legends of the Canopy Canines

In the canopy high, where the canines play,
Tales of mischief brighten the day.
With wagging tails and plenty of bark,
They leap and tumble, leaving a mark!

The sunbeams dance on their furry backs,
As they sniff and wag, living life tall.
Each yip and howl tells a wild tale,
Of legendary games on a leafy trail.

From chasing the wind to stealing a shoe,
These playful poets write stories anew.
Every bark a chapter, every wag a rhyme,
Their laughter rings out like sweet nursery chime.

So join the fun in this forested realm,
Where tales take flight and joy overwhelms.
In the hearts of canines, legends unfold,
Of laughter and friendship, forever retold!

Melodies of the Moonlit Grove

In the glow of the night sky,
Frogs croak a goofy tune,
Owls wink with a sly eye,
Squirrels dance by the moon.

The fireflies start to giggle,
While shadows swing and sway,
Raccoons join in the wiggle,
As night steals the day away.

Underneath the old tall trees,
The whispers tickle the leaves,
As raccoons share wild stories,
Of silly tricks up their sleeves.

With laughter woven in song,
And stars scattered all around,
In this grove, we all belong,
Where joy is truly profound.

Tales from the Tree-Top Haven

High above in branches wide,
Birds chirp in perfect rhyme,
Squirrels munch on nuts with pride,
The sunlight welcomes the climb.

A chattering crew of critters,
Telling tales of great delight,
With antics that surely fitters,
Dancing 'til they lose the light.

The parrot paints with bright hues,
As raccoons spin clumsy tales,
Each laugh a hilarious bruise,
While mockingbirds mimic the gales.

In a tree-top world so grand,
Where every nutty jest plays,
The woodlands clap, an applause band,
For friendship's joyful displays.

Harmonies of the Hidden Hollow

In a hollow tucked away,
Where the mushrooms giggle loud,
The hedgehogs sing all day,
While crickets croon, quite proud.

Amidst the ferns and wild blooms,
Where the brook bubbles with cheer,
Each creature shares their cartoon,
Making nonsense crystal clear.

A deer prances with comic flair,
While the rabbits start a race,
With a skip and a funny glare,
They leap in a joyful chase.

Echoing in the green bower,
Sweet chaos fills the air,
In this anthem of pure power,
There's laughter everywhere.

Chants of the Twilight Thicket

As twilight drapes the thicket,
Critters gather with delight,
A beaver's building crickets,
While fireflies dance in flight.

The bunnies hop in a tune,
Chasing each other in glee,
The raccoon plays out of tune,
With a splash from the nearby sea.

Giggling badgers join in song,
They narrate tales of the night,
In this gathering all along,
Fun emerges, pure and bright.

With nightfall, the antics swell,
In shadows, they prance about,
Under their own bright spell,
Where silly dreams drive the rout.

Aria of Dappled Shadows

In a forest where the sun plays,
Silly squirrels dance in a haze.
Chasing their tails with boundless glee,
A show of acorns, their grand decree.

The branches sway with laughter loud,
While frolicsome frogs form a crowd.
Their ribbits echo, a comical tune,
As shadows chuckle beneath the moon.

A bumblebee hums a jolly old song,
While a lazy bear rolls with a yawn.
The rustling leaves, a playful tease,
Nature's delight puts our hearts at ease.

With dappled light, the day comes to end,
As funny creatures, to dreams, they bend.
In a world where giggles take the lead,
Life's a melody, indeed, indeed!

Songs from the Heartwood

Whispers of saplings, oh what a sight,
Their stories unfold with pure delight.
A chipmunk sneezes, a comical sound,
As giggles and chuckles start to rebound.

Twisting tendrils of ivy insist,
They'll have you blushing, you get the gist.
With a tickle of leaves on a breezy day,
Nature's mischief is here to stay.

Where laughter and light intertwine like vines,
The trees gossip with quirky designs.
A quirky woodpecker knocks on bark,
Playing tunes that spark a lark!

In each crevice, a surprise waits,
On branches where humor often debates.
The heartwood sings of antics so grand,
In a world where joy takes a stand.

Rhythms of the Whispering Breeze

A gentle breeze rolls through the trees,
Dancing with leaves as if to tease.
The petals flutter, a jazzy ballet,
While critters carouse in an amusing fray.

Each gust brings a whisper, a chuckle refined,
With giggling grasses that swirl unconfined.
The sunbeams tickle their bouncy heads,
While creeping shadows race under beds.

Squirrels giggle as they flip and glide,
And wise old owls join in for the ride.
With every rustle, a new tale resumes,
In the land of laughter, where silliness blooms.

The wind carries secrets in playful delight,
As nature unfolds, painting the night.
In rhythms of whimsy, the world spins around,
A tapestry woven with fun's merry sound.

The Poetry of Knotted Branches

Underneath the twisted limbs of yore,
Lie tales of antics, waiting to soar.
An owl in glasses reads the news,
Of shy rabbits and their colorful views.

Branches shake with laughter and mirth,
As squirrels hold a feast, down to earth.
Exchange of snacks, a trade of delight,
While the sun dips slowly, dimming the light.

The knotted trunks stand firm and proud,
As whispers and giggles gather a crowd.
A chubby raccoon, with a wink and a grin,
Shares candy wrappers he stashed deep within.

With every knot, there's a story to tell,
Of friendships found and the times they fell.
In this quirky bower, joy's here to stay,
A living poem in its own playful way.

Lullabies in the Underbrush

In the thicket, critters hum,
A chorus soft, it's quite the fun.
With fluffy tails and sleepy eyes,
They dream of pies in starry skies.

Swaying leaves join in delight,
As fireflies blink through the night.
A raccoon plays a tiny flute,
While frogs tap dance in a cute suit.

The owls hoot a lullaby call,
Crickets chirp, it's a jamboree ball.
In every nook, wonders await,
Underbrush tales, it's never too late.

So snuggle tight, let dreams take flight,
In this funny land, all feels right.
Adventure waits in the morning light,
With giggles echoing in the night.

The Rhythm of Twisting Vines

Twisting vines dance in the sun,
Branches sway, oh what fun!
A squirrel spins, with flair and style,
He flips and flaps, all the while.

Laughter fills the leafy air,
A parrot squawks without a care.
The bumblebees hum catchy tunes,
Under the watchful eye of moons.

Every twist brings a surprise,
Frogs leap high, they touch the skies.
And as the wind begins to play,
Nature's orchestra sings away.

So join the dance in this wild space,
With furry friends in a merry race.
The rhythm calls, don't be shy,
Come twist along and say hi!

Odes to the Wooden Giants

Oh mighty trees, so tall and grand,
With wooden arms, they take a stand.
Whispers swirl in their leafy crown,
Tickling the noses of creatures 'round.

From chipmunk chatter to crow's caw,
Every branch holds quirky law.
They giggle as the wind rolls by,
Their sturdy trunks, the clouds up high.

Knots of wisdom, tales they weave,
Of acorns dropped and webs we leave.
In their shade, secrets unfold,
Funny stories just waiting to be told.

So raise a cheer to the ancient bark,
In forest's heart, life leaves its mark.
Stand in awe, or join the play,
With wooden giants, we'll laugh all day!

Chronicles of the Leafy Realm

In the leafy realm where dreams take flight,
Wiggly worms write tales of delight.
A leaf spins like a tiny disc,
While rabbits ponder, 'What's for brisk?'

Mice hold court with a toad's advice,
"Dance with the raindrops, so very nice!"
Dewdrops giggle, sunsbeam grin,
In this realm, everyone fits in.

A hedgehog recites a poet's verse,
A funny tale, oh how it's terse!
With every giggle, the flowers sway,
In rhymes and laughter, they play all day.

So gather round beneath the trees,
Join the fun with the buzzing bees.
In the leafy realm, let's all proclaim,
Adventures await, let's play the game!

Ballads of the Boughs and Breezes

In leafy realms where giggles grow,
The branches dance, the breezes blow.
A squirrel sings its choppy tune,
While ants march under sun and moon.

A parrot laughs at all the rest,
It thinks it's truly the beast best.
With leafy hats and acorn crowns,
They prance and play with cheeky frowns.

The wind tells tales of twirls and whirls,
While butterflies wear sparkling pearls.
A jumpy frog in rhymes does leap,
While nearby trees all laugh and peep.

So here we cheer for nature's jest,
In joyful boughs, we find our rest.
With giggles sprouting from the ground,
In breezes' laughter, joy is found.

Chronicles of the Climbing Vines

Upon the trellis, laughter clings,
As curious vines do funny things.
They stretch and twirl — oh what a sight!
In playful fights, they wrestle light.

The grape has jokes, it tells them sweet,
As leaves drop down like quickened feet.
They tangle up in giggles fine,
While crickets chirp in twisted line.

A wobbly gourd rolls down the way,
It wishes for a game to play.
With sunflower hats, so bold and bright,
They twirl and tease till day turns night.

In laughter's grip, they sway and strive,
The garden thrives, so full of life.
With every tendril's twist and bend,
The charming vines are laughter's blend.

Odes to the Orchard's Echo

Beneath the trees, the laughter rings,
Where apples jump and swing their flings.
A hen's clucks echo, loud and clear,
While pigs roll 'round without a fear.

Each fruit has jokes to tell and share,
As pears discuss the windswept air.
With every rustle, giggles break,
While nature's toys begin to quake.

The oranges throw a roundabout,
While plums play chase, there's never doubt.
In this fairground of tree and vine,
The orchard hums a voice divine.

So lift your glass, let laughter pour,
In echoes rich, let spirit soar.
In every bite, a joke awaits,
A feast of giggles on our plates.

Murmurs of the Misty Moor

In misty realms where giggles glide,
The whispers tease, they run and hide.
With frolicking foxes, stories bloom,
Amusing thoughts from every zoom.

A hare hops high, it pulls a prank,
While mushrooms chuckle on the bank.
Their caps all shake in laughter's trance,
As shadows twirl in playful dance.

The fog rolls in with tales untold,
Of pixie tricks and elfin gold.
They titter 'neath the silver moon,
While sowing seeds of bright festoon.

So heed the murmurs of this field,
In humor's grasp, all hearts are healed.
In nature's laughter, we converse,
A merry moor, a happy verse.

www.ingramcontent.com/pod-product-compliance
Lightning Source LLC
Chambersburg PA
CBHW071831160426
43209CB00003B/274